How do you see the world?

Also by Alis Rowe

One Lonely Mind
978-0-9562693-0-0

The Girl With The Curly Hair - Asperger's and Me
978-0-9562693-2-4

The 1st Comic Book
978-0-9562693-1-7

The 2nd Comic Book
978-0-9562693-4-8

The 3rd Comic Book
978-0-9562693-3-1

The 4th Comic Book
978-15086839-7-1

The 5th Comic Book
978-15309879-3-1

Websites:
www.thegirlwiththecurlyhair.co.uk
www.thecurlyhairconsultancy.com
www.theliftingplace.com

Social Media:
www.facebook.com/thegirlwiththecurlyhair
www.twitter.com/curlyhairedalis

Develop greater ability to put yourself in someone else's shoes and enjoy more successful relationships

Lonely Mind Books
London

Copyrighted Material

Published by
Lonely Mind Books
London

Copyright © Alis Rowe 2018

For individuals, friends, parents, managers, teachers, students, children... for everyone!

Contents

hello

The Girl With The Curly Hair has Asperger's Syndrome (an Autism Spectrum Disorder/ASD). It doesn't especially matter that she has Asperger's Syndrome. To you the reader, all that matters is for you to try to think about how each character in each scenario might be feeling and why, and how it might be best for them to respond to each other (assuming they're both fantastic at putting themselves in each other's shoes!).

The purpose of this book is to help you to be more understanding and accepting of someone who is different to you.

What is empathy?

Empathy can be described as feeling what someone else is feeling.

A person might be empathetic once they have identified the thoughts and feelings of someone else.

A lot of people think that they are good at putting themselves in other people's shoes and therefore believe that they are empathetic.

However, most people get the idea of being in another person's shoes wrong. A more effective way of relating to someone else is to put yourself in their shoes as though you were them, not as though they were you (which is what most people tend to do).

Reflect upon the following scenarios and consider whether any of the characters involved could show more empathy.

Consider whether it's any different if we know a person well versus we don't know them well at all (our own thinking is that if a person knows someone else well they have more chance of being empathetic).

Think about why it's important to tell other people what we are thinking and how we are feeling. We think that if we are open and tell people, the other person will have more of a chance of being empathetic.

The park

The Girl With The Curly Hair and her sister are about to go out. It's Sunday. They always go to the park on a Sunday.

How might her sister be feeling?
How might The Girl With The Curly Hair be feeling?
Would it help The Girl With The Curly Hair if her sister
had explained why she wanted to go bowling?
Why might it be important to The Girl With The Curly
Hair to always go to the park on Sundays?
Why might her sister want to go bowling?

Consider why some people like routine.

Meeting up at the weekend

The Girl With The Curly Hair is invited to see her friend at the weekend.

Would there have been a more sensitive way for The Girl With The Curly Hair to have responded?

How might The Girl With The Curly Hair's friend have felt?

Why might the friend have made an assumption that The Girl With The Curly Hair doesn't like her?

How might The Girl With The Curly Hair have felt after her friend responds?

Would there have been a more empathetic way for her friend to have responded?

Think about how different people like to spend their free time.

Veterinary surgery reception

The Girl With The Curly Hair works on Reception with two colleagues in a busy veterinary surgery.

How might The Girl With The Curly Hair's colleagues have been feeling?

What did The Girl With The Curly Hair do differently to them?

How might The Girl With The Curly Hair be feeling listening to her colleagues?

Consider how some people are more adaptive to making suggestions and change whilst others might not be.

A small, local university

The Girl With The Curly Hair has applied to go to a small, local university. She tells the teacher she's going to live at home and the other students overhear.

Why might The Girl With The Curly Hair not want to move away?

Why might The Girl With The Curly Hair want to live at home?

Why might the other students want to move away and live somewhere new?

Why might a teacher want The Girl With The Curly Hair to go to a different university?

Why do the other students and the teacher challenge her decision?

How might what they are all saying be making The Girl With The Curly Hair feel?

How could they have been more empathetic?

Consider why it might be important to respect the decision that someone else has made.

3pm meeting

The Girl With The Curly Hair has arranged to meet her friend at 3p.m.

How might The Girl With The Curly Hair be feeling during these 6 minutes?

How might what The Girl With The Curly Hair first says make her friend feel?

Why doesn't The Girl With The Curly Hair initially answer her friend's question, "How are you doing?"

Why doesn't her friend initially acknowledge that he is late?

Why doesn't her friend answer her question and tell her why he is late?

What tone might this dialogue cause the rest of their meeting to be like?

Consider why punctuality might be so important to some people.

Watching TV

The Girl With The Curly Hair is watching TV with her friends.

Why might the sound be too loud for The Girl With The Curly Hair but not her friends?

How might The Girl With The Curly Hair be feeling when she asks them to turn the volume down?

How might The Girl With The Curly Hair be feeling once the volume has been turned down, yet it's still too loud?

Why is The Girl With The Curly Hair unsure how to ask them to turn the volume down again?

What would be a good way for her to ask them a second time?

What would be an empathetic way for them to respond?

Think about which 'normal' daily experiences can make you feel physically uncomfortable.

Eggs for breakfast

The Girl With The Curly Hair is cooking eggs for her husband to have for breakfast.

Why might The Girl With The Curly Hair's husband not mind how he has his eggs?

Or does he mind? But chooses not to say so - if so, why might he not state his preference?

How might The Girl With The Curly Hair feel when he says he doesn't mind?

Why might she not understand why he says he doesn't mind?

How might her husband feel about her cooking breakfast for him?

Consider how different people have strong preferences for certain things, and others care less.

Pull your socks up

The Girl With The Curly Hair is in a lesson. The teacher asks the class to "pull your socks up." The Girl With The Curly Hair bends down and pulls her socks up.

Why does the teacher use this funny saying?

What does this saying mean?

Why does The Girl With The Curly Hair pull her socks up?

What might the other students feel about The Girl With The Curly Hair when she does this?

How might the other students laughing make The Girl With The Curly Hair feel?

What might the teacher be thinking when she sees The Girl With The Curly Hair pulling her socks up?

What else could the teacher have said or done?

Consider the impact on other people of funny sayings that we might use.

An extended deadline

All The Girl With The Curly Hair's classmates haven't done their homework, so the teacher decides to extend the deadline.

Why might the teacher have extended the deadline?

How might this homework extension make the other students feel?

Why did none of the other students do their homework?

How might the extension of the deadline make The Girl With The Curly Hair feel about herself, about the teacher, about the other students, and about the situation generally?

Why might she have been the only one to complete the homework?

Consider what the purpose of deadlines are and why they are important.

New starter

A new starter has been at her new job for a week.

How might the new starter be feeling about her new job and her colleagues?

How might the manager be feeling about the new starter?

How might The Girl With The Curly Hair be feeling about the new starter?

How might the new starter be feeling after The Girl With The Curly Hair has offered her some help?

How might The Girl With The Curly Hair have felt after helping the new starter?

How might the manager have felt about The Girl With The Curly Hair helping the new starter?

Think about what it's like when we go or start something new or when we meet new people and how it can sometimes be hard to fit in.

Chemistry

It's the Chemistry lesson.

How might the teacher be feeling about this work and her students?

How might the students be feeling about this work?

How might the students be feeling in response to what the teacher says?

How might The Girl With The Curly Hair be feeling in response to what the teacher says?

How could the teacher have more empathy for The Girl With The Curly Hair?

Think about situations you know where different people find similar tasks both easy and hard, and consider how similar tasks could be adapted for different people.

Cup of tea or a walk?

The Girl With The Curly Hair meets up with a friend.

How might The Girl With The Curly Hair be feeling when her friend says this?

Why might her friend not want to have a cup of tea in the cafe as they had planned?

Why might The Girl With The Curly Hair want to have a cup of tea in the cafe?

How could the friend have been more empathetic?

If The Girl With The Curly Hair doesn't want to go for a walk, how might she say so whilst sensitively considering his feelings?

Consider how we can learn to tell people what we want without upsetting them.

GP Reception

The Girl With The Curly Hair is waiting at the front of the queue at the GP Reception.

Why might the Receptionist not acknowledge The Girl With The Curly Hair?

How might The Girl With The Curly Hair be feeling when she first arrives at the front of the queue?

How might she be feeling 6 minutes later?

Why might The Girl With The Curly Hair not know what to do or say?

How could the Receptionist have been more considerate of The Girl With The Curly Hair?

Consider the importance of acknowledging others and being friendly.

Blood pressure

The Girl With The Curly Hair is about to have her blood pressure taken.

How might The Girl With The Curly Hair have felt, saying this to the nurse?

How might the nurse feel when The Girl With The Curly Hair says this?

How might the nurse's response make The Girl With The Curly Hair feel?

What could the nurse have said to be a bit more empathetic?

Consider how different people might need different things to help them cope.

08:11 train

The Girl With The Curly Hair is waiting for the 08:11 train to arrive. There is another person on the platform.

Has the other person noticed the sign and the time?
If he has, why isn't he thinking about it?
Why might The Girl With The Curly Hair be focused on the sign and the time?
Why might The Girl With The Curly Hair be worrying that she's going to be late for work?
Why might the other person not be worrying about being late for work?

Consider how different people feel about things not running to time.

Expensive shoes

The Girl With The Curly Hair is chatting with her friends.

Why might the other girls be interested in having expensive shoes?

How might the other girls be feeling as they are discussing the shoes?

How might The Girl With The Curly Hair be feeling when her friends are talking about the shoes?

Why might The Girl With The Curly Hair be thinking about her friend's language?

Why might The Girl With The Curly Hair use the same language?

Think about when we sometimes say things we don't really mean and why we do this.

Side salad

The Girl With The Curly Hair orders her usual side salad at the restaurant.

How might The Girl With The Curly Hair be feeling when she receives her side salad?
Why might the chef have put pepper on her side salad?
Why might The Girl With The Curly Hair not want to ask for her side salad to be returned herself?
How might her husband be feeling when she asks this?
How might The Girl With The Curly Hair be feeling about her husband's reply?
Could her husband have responded in a more empathetic way?

Consider that what you might think is unimportant might be very important for someone else.

Reading out loud

The Girl With The Curly Hair is in an English lesson.
The teacher has asked the class to take turns to read
out loud from the book they are studying.

Why might The Girl With The Curly Hair not want to read out loud?

Why might The Girl With The Curly Hair not be able to speak when it's her turn?

How might The Girl With The Curly Hair be feeling when she's not able to speak?

How might the teacher be feeling about The Girl With The Curly Hair when this happens?

What might the classmates be thinking and feeling about The Girl With The Curly Hair when this happens?

How could the teacher have been more empathetic?

Consider how people behave when they are anxious.

Class Registration

The Girl With The Curly Hair is in Class Registration. It's the end of the school day.

Why might the class be chatting so much?

Why doesn't the teacher want to keep the class behind?

Why might the teacher not think to let The Girl With The Curly Hair go?

How might The Girl With The Curly Hair be feeling when the teacher threatens to keep the class behind?

Could the teacher be more empathetic to The Girl With The Curly Hair?

Consider how different people might feel at the end of a school day.

Promotion

The Girl With The Curly Hair has been asked by her Manager whether she wants to be promoted to a new role that is much better paid.

Why might her Manager want The Girl With The Curly Hair to take this new role?

Why does her Manager assume that The Girl With The Curly Hair will be pleased?

How might The Girl With The Curly Hair be feeling when her Manager asks?

Why might The Girl With The Curly Hair not want the new role?

How might her Manager feel when she says no?

Think about why it is that some people assume you want what they would like.

Corn flakes

The Girl With The Curly Hair is in the kitchen with her Dad. It is breakfast time. She looks for her normal corn flakes.

How might Dad first be feeling knowing that he has bought corn flakes for The Girl With The Curly Hair?

How might Dad feel when The Girl With The Curly Hair just asks where her normal corn flakes are?

How might The Girl With The Curly Hair be feeling when Dad says "That's all they had. They're all the same anyway"?

How might Dad be feeling when The Girl With The Curly Hair responds in the way that she does?

Could The Girl With The Curly Hair have been more sensitive with Dad? If so, how?

Could Dad have been more empathetic with The Girl With The Curly Hair? If so, how?

Discuss why it might be important to acknowledge someone who has tried to help in a situation as best they can.

The doorbell rings

The Girl With The Curly Hair's doorbell rings. It's one of her good friends.

How might the friend have felt ringing on The Girl With The Curly Hair's door?

How might The Girl With The Curly Hair have felt when she answered the door?

Why might The Girl With The Curly Hair not have wanted to chat?

If The Girl With The Curly Hair didn't want to chat, what could she have said to be sensitive to her friend?

Discuss how different people might feel about spontaneous interaction.

Hot weather

The Girl With The Curly Hair is out walking. She bumps into someone.

How might the person feel when The Girl With The Curly Hair tells her she prefers the winter?

How might The Girl With The Curly Hair feel when the person replies in this way?

How could the other person have been more empathetic?

Consider how different people experience weather.

After college

The Girl With The Curly Hair has arrived home from college. Her classmate texts her.

Why might her classmate still be at college when The Girl With The Curly Hair is already at home?

How might The Girl With The Curly Hair be feeling when she reads his text?

Why might her classmate want to see The Girl With The Curly Hair instead of going home?

Why might her classmate not be worried about his coursework?

Consider what priorities different people have.

B.A.N.A.N.A.

The Girl With The Curly Hair is on the train.

*The Girl With The Curly Hair finds the smell of bananas overpowering and unpleasant. Other people might find foods such as fish or curry overpowering.

Why might The Girl With The Curly Hair feel she has to move carriage?
Why might the person be eating a banana on the train?
Was the person being inconsiderate?

Consider the impact of our actions on others when we are in a public place.

Osteopath

The Girl With The Curly Hair is at the osteopath.

Why might The Girl With The Curly Hair prefer to make appointments via email?
Why might the osteopathy clinic not reply to emails?
Why might the osteopath assume that making calls is "the easiest way"?
How might the osteopath's response make The Girl With The Curly Hair feel?
What could he have said instead?

Think about the different methods of communication (such as telephone and email) and why someone might prefer one over another.

The community fair

The Girl With The Curly Hair arrives at the local community fair. Her workplace have a stand and she had agreed to help out.

How might The Girl With The Curly Hair feel when she turns up and sees Sarah?

How might her colleague be feeling having managed to get Sarah to help out?

How might Sarah be feeling about helping out?

Consider how some people's actions can have unintended consequences on those involved.

Working from home

The Girl With The Curly Hair asks her Boss if she can start working from home more often.

Why might The Girl With The Curly Hair want to work from home more often?

How might her Boss's response make The Girl With The Curly Hair feel?

How important is it that The Girl With The Curly Hair explains why she wants to work from home?

Consider the different ways that people work best.

Listening to music

The Girl With The Curly Hair is listening to music with her friend.

Why might The Girl With The Curly Hair think and talk about the song lyrics?

Why might her friend not have noticed the song lyrics?

What might her friend like about listening to music?

Consider how different people can have the same interests but like different aspects.

Their and They're error

The Girl With The Curly Hair is in a meeting at work. They're all discussing how to make customer service even better. The meeting presenter is using a flipchart.

Why might the meeting presenter have made this error?
Why might The Girl With The Curly Hair be focusing on this error?
Has anyone else noticed? If so, why might no one have mentioned it? Has the meeting presenter noticed? If so, why might she not have corrected it?
What if no one has noticed this error... why might they not have?

Think about situations in which good attention to detail is helpful and situations where it might not be.

Always remember that everyone is different

How do YOU see the world?

About Alis Rowe

The Girl With The Curly Hair is an autistic character strongly based on the well known author and real life entrepreneur, Alis Rowe.

Alis's work is all about understanding different perspectives and appreciating that not everyone is the same and that being different is not necessarily wrong. Indeed, difference can be amazing!

A person who is different can have many positive traits, which can be very, very useful once they are understood.

Find out more about Alis's powerful, innovative, "life changing" work at

www.thegirlwiththecurlyhair.co.uk

Printed in Germany
by Amazon Distribution
GmbH, Leipzig